37 TIPS & TOOLS:
TO HELP YOU IMPRESS YOUR BOSS

To my patient and understanding partner, thank you for playing the devil's advocate and keeping my feet firmly on the ground. To my darling son . . . thank you for making me laugh.

To my family, mentors and colleagues, thank you for continuing to be my inspiration and a special thank you to my editor, Renée Jasen, for her attention to detail and valuable suggestions.

37 TIPS & TOOLS:
TO HELP YOU IMPRESS YOUR BOSS

TRACEY B ABELL

ISBN: 978-0-9943-0460-5

National Library of Australia
Cataloguing-in-Publication Data

Author:	Abell, Tracey B
Title:	37 Tips & Tools: To Help You Impress Your Boss
Edition:	1st ed.
ISBN:	9780994304605 (paperback)
Notes:	Includes bibliography
Subjects:	Management - - Handbooks, manuals, etc.
	Business communication
	Teams in the workplace
	Time management
Dewey Number:	658

Contents

Preface

Welcome to 37 *Tips & Tools: To Help You Impress Your Boss*.

I am a company Director and have been engaged to manage staff for many years. It is a passion of mine to help my team members improve both their skills and output, while at the same time reducing their levels of work-related stress and frustration.

As a business educator, I have trained thousands of people in both business and project management skills. Sadly, it is my experience that most business and project management tools are overly complex and thus rarely used effectively.

I am driven to change this because I believe that everyone deserves the opportunity to be more successful, more easily. Whoever said that life wasn't meant to be easy was doing things the hard way!

This book takes 37 tools and tips that my team has used successfully in our projects and operations, and presents them in clear, concise and useable manner, that can be applied to virtually any role in any industry.

I would also like to invite you to discover even more beneficial skills and techniques you can learn through our YouTube Channel (Tracey Abell), our complimentary webinars (www.developmental.com.au/ events.html) and our 3 day Conference and Workshop (www.developmental.com.au/conference.html).

Introduction

Imagine if you could improve your work output at the same time as reducing your stress and improving your work life balance.

It's a crazy notion isn't it? But let me assure you that <u>it is entirely possible</u>.

A commonly held belief in the business world is that:

Work = Output

Do you agree?

Have you ever worked with 'that person' who works long hours every day but hardly ever completes anything?   And when they do, the results are often substandard anyway!

People like that are proof that creating output does not necessarily guarantee the achievement of Key Performance Indicators (KPIs) or fulfilling their job description.

I like to think of my team's work equation as:

Smart Work = Quality and Timely Output

And it is my responsibility as a Manager to help them achieve the output targets I have set for them.

My core business focuses on Project Management and educating people working in the project management field.

This has provided me with years of experience seeing people '*doing things the hard way*', and watching them become more and more stressed and frustrated, ultimately affecting personal and workplace morale and even their health and home life.

The project management tools that I teach people about apply just as effectively in any business role. Managing a project is about working with others on a one-time event or activity, to produce a predetermined outcome, within a set period of time.

It is different from day-to-day working life, as a project has a pre-defined time period, whereas day to day work (generally) has no defined end date. It just goes on and on and on. . .

There are a number of key areas that apply to running a project which are also central to effective business operations. The diagram below demonstrates this:

The upcoming chapters will explore each category shown in this diagram and provide handy tips to improve your work output whiles reducing your stress and improving your work life balance.

If you are too busy to read this book, at least take the time on your next coffee break to look at the pictures. Those alone could save you hours each week.

A small investment for a massive return!

Chapter 1: Managing Your Time

Time Management is the ability to structure your available time in a manner that allows effective completion of required activities. I know what you might be thinking . . ."*There is never enough time in my day*".

There are nearly always opportunities to improve time management in a day. Here are a few simple ones that you may be able to apply right now:

1. **ONLY CHECK YOUR EMAILS THREE TIMES A DAY** - morning, after lunch and about 1 hour before your set finish time. Something to consider is notifying people of the time of the day that you check emails by adding it to your email signature. That way people can call you instead of emailing you if a matter is extremely urgent. Turn the automatic notifications off in your email settings so that you are not constantly bombarded with the incoming emails. You can save over an hour each day by doing this.

2. **CATEGORISE AND SORT YOUR EMAILS** – Create folders in your email system for each day of the week, as well as a folder for next week, and a folder for each month of the year. You

will then have 18 folders with the following labels:

- Monday, Tuesday, Wednesday, Thursday, Friday
- Next Week
- January, February, March, April, May, June, July, August, September, October, November and December.

Set aside into the appropriate folder anything that does not need to be dealt with immediately and stay away from it until you either have spare time available, or the scheduled time arrives for you to commence the work.

3. **STOP PROCRASTINATING** – This old chestnut, right? We all have tasks that we don't want to do, for many reasons. My suggestion is that after you check your emails and handle any urgent work, you tackle *'that'* task. Give yourself a set time period (such as one hour) and work hard at it for the entire time. Set an alarm on your phone or computer, then, when the time is up, go and have a short break. After that, you can get on with the rest of your day.

Set aside the same amount of time each day until the task is finished and the stress of this job *'hanging over your head'* is gone from your work life.

4. **MAKE THE MOST OF YOUR PRIME TIME** - Everyone has their own energy cycle. Some people bound out of bed at 5am, go for a jog, and turn up at work ready to go. Others take three cups of coffee and don't get going until 10am, but they really work well after that. Find out when you work most effectively, and try to organise these times so that you can avoid interruptions. Schedule the work that takes the most thought at this time of day, while you are at your best.

5. **MINIMISE MULTI-TASKING** – When you split your attention between multiple tasks, you create a mental traffic jam and nothing gets done well. This can actually reduce your performance by up to 40%.

6. **PACIFY PAPERWORK** – Throw away what you don't need on your desk (assuming you can get it elsewhere if you need it – such as the company intranet or the filing cabinet). This is also a great time to de-clutter your desk. It is a cleansing experience and creates a positive work environment.

7. **RESTRICT INTERRUPTIONS** - Interruptions can eat away at your day and exhaust you. Consider working while everyone else is on

their lunch break and have your break later. This will also help the afternoon to go by faster.

8. **BREAK DOWN BIG TASKS** - If you have a task that requires a lot of time and effort, you may say, *"oh, I won't start that now, or I'll have to leave halfway through"*. Most of the time, you could break the big task into 10 smaller ones, and could knock off part of it every afternoon. With this approach, you will find that the task is complete in no time. Create an action plan and schedule block-out times into your diary so you have no (or limited) interruptions while you are working on it. See Chapter 3 for details on how to do this.

9. **CHANGE YOUR MINDSET** - Feel the fear and do it anyway - it is so empowering! Change your mindset and think of daunting tasks as learning opportunities. Is it fear of failure or fear of success that gets in your way? Give yourself permission to succeed and get that task done.

10. **TAME THE TELEPHONE** - If you work in sales and customer service, the telephone is a necessary measure, but you can try to set your phone to your message service for one or two hours each day so that you can really concentrate. Combine this with your prime time and you will be amazed at the difference.

Immediately you have 10 tips and tools that you can use to improve time management (and help save your sanity).

I have saved the best until last (*almost last*) – it is one of my favourites and has had the biggest impact on improving time management for myself and my team.

Using Brainstorming To Develop An Effective To-Do List

Brainstorming is when you list every idea that you have about what needs to be done for your job. The ideas 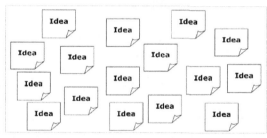 are not validated at this point, they are simply listed.

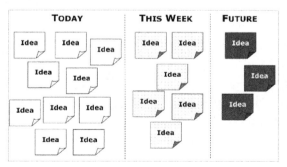 A useful tip is to write each idea on a sticky-note, or use mind mapping software and put each idea in its own text box. The purpose of this is to

enable you to reorganise the ideas later, without having to continuously rewrite them.

This activity may take you 10 minutes to complete, but could save you up to an hour in wasted time later. You then need to categorise your ideas so that you can plan your work flow for the day, week, fortnight or month.

The next step is to prioritise today's ideas:

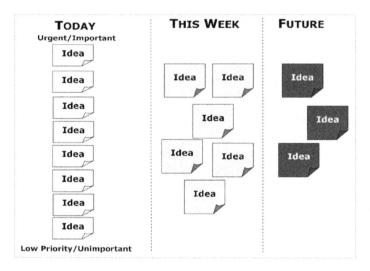

Then enter them into your To-Do List or Outlook calendar and tick them off as you go. Review them again just prior to lunch time and re-evaluate the prioritisation.

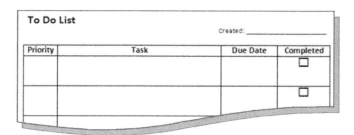

A FEW MORE TIPS:

1. **GO FOR SOME COLOUR** - If you use a paper To-Do list (and yes, I still do), print it on brightly coloured paper. That way you can always find it no matter how messy your desk is.

2. **TRANSFER AND FILE** - At the end of the day, transfer any remaining tasks onto tomorrow's list (or drag and drop in Outlook) and file the To-Do list away. Do NOT throw the old list away or shred it as this becomes a catalogue of your work and a very important reference point.

3. **DO YOUR PLANNING THE DAY BEFORE** – At the end of the day, about 15 minutes before you grab your keys and lunch box and run for the door – stop working! Prepare your To-Do list for tomorrow, making sure you transfer over any emails from the Outlook folder that you created for tomorrow's work (see page 11, point 2). There are two reasons for this:

- Firstly, your brain is probably only firing on half a cylinder at this point in time, so you may as well stop doing work that you could damage and have to redo tomorrow anyway, and gain some value out of the time.

- Secondly, being organised ahead of time gives you peace of mind so you can get a good night's sleep, and come to work the next day without any panic or confusion on what you should be working on.

Chapter Summary

Have you ever heard the old adage below?

"Failing to Plan
is Planning to Fail"

The above tips and tools will help you avoid failure to plan and generate a higher output through your work day with the added bonus of less stress. You can even try them at home for that long list of tasks that never seems to get done!

Could you ask for more?

(If your answer is yes – read on to Chapter 2!)

Chapter 2: Effective Communication

'Communication' is a word thrown around every day, if not every minute, in the world of business. My experience is that most people do not actually understand it, and those that do still do not communicate effectively.

So, what is communication?

In the book, *Organisational Behaviour - Core Concepts and Applications (Fitzgerald et al. 2006)*, organisational communication is defined as:

> *"The process by which entities exchange information and establish a common understanding."*

The diagram below represents this process:

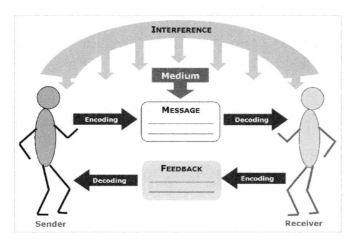

Sender

The exchange of information in the communication process occurs when one person (the Sender) composes a message and sends it to another person or people (the Receiver/s).

Effective communication may begin to be impeded even at this early stage in the communication process.

The Sender has a range of experience and knowledge that is different to everyone else. This is due to their life and work background, education, culture and a range of other factors. When the Sender composes the message, they do something called 'Encoding'. Encoding means that the Sender phrases and structures the communication using their unique knowledge, experience and language.

Receiver

The Receiver then needs to 'Decode' the message so that they can respond and provide some kind of feedback. This feedback may be verbal, non-verbal or documented.

A communication 'Medium' can refer to a wide range of things including:

- Email or other internet/online communication

- Intranet communication tools
- Letter
- Memo
- Fax (does anyone still use this?)
- Telephone or mobile phone call
- Report
- Information documentation such as a brochure
- Meeting agenda or minutes
- Plans, specifications and data sheets
- Policies and procedures
- Face to face meeting, such as a toolbox or staff meeting
- Survey
- Workshop or presentation.

'*Interference*' is a term used to encapsulate anything that may affect the communication process, such as:

- Background noise
- Interference with technology (such as a phone line dropping out)
- Hearing or speaking difficulties
- Extreme temperature or weather
- Technology failure
- Remote location issues
- Incomplete documentation
- Learning styles
- Personality conflicts
- Attitude towards work or others
- Behavioural issues

- Alcohol or medication
- Medical issues
- Other problems outside of the communication situation

Strategies to Maximise the Communication Process:

1. **Understand the Receiver** – The person (or people) that you are communicating with have a unique set of characteristics, skills, knowledge and experience. If you have an understanding of these, you can communicate in a manner that ensures they can understand the message.

2. **Carefully select the medium** – The content and Receiver of the message will influence the medium you select. If you are providing a complex list of instructions, email may be most appropriate, however if you are communicating with someone at a remote site with intermittent internet, there may be a better method.

3. **Check for understanding** – It is important to ensure the Receiver clearly and comprehensively understands the message you are sending to allow them to act on it. You should check they are in fact clear on the details and that they will act in an appropriate way.

4. **AVOID INTERFERENCE FACTORS** – Think about what factors could interfere with your communication process. Are you dealing with someone working in a loud location or someone with restrictions on what they can receive by email? Consider all of the issues that could interfere with the effective receipt of your message and minimise them wherever possible.

5. **BE AWARE OF FEEDBACK** - You will always receive feedback from the Receiver of your message. It is important to note that this feedback may be in the form of silence. Silence from the Receiver can mean many things, including their confusion over your message or failure to receive all or part of the message. If you are faced with silence, follow up and resolve any issues affecting the process.

6. **TAKE CARE WHEN ENCODING YOUR MESSAGE** – The encoding you use within the messages you send will directly impact on the effective receipt of that message. Simple cause and effect. If the Receiver does not understand you, they cannot act and the entire communication process is wasted.

Poor communication and a range of other factors

may result in conflict between yourself and others, or between other team members. This is not conducive to an effective working environment.

A conflict is any significant difference of opinion. It does not need to involve anger, or worse still, violence.

Conflict makes for an uncomfortable workplace and can create unnecessary stress and damage workforce morale.

TIPS TO HELP MANAGE WORKPLACE CONFLICT:

1. **BE THE *'BIGGER PERSON'*** – Sometimes it is necessary to walk away from a conflict situation to avoid escalation. It is important that the other party does not think you are *'ignoring them'*. If possible, let them know you can see you are at odds with each other and that you do not want to escalate the conflict. Make them feel reassured that you will revisit the situation at a later date or time and in a more comfortable environment.

2. **CHECK FOR UNDERSTANDING** – If you are at odds with someone (or a group of people), ask questions to check that you are in fact referring to the same situation or case, and check that everyone has all of the facts. Conflict is difficult to manage if based on rumour or innuendo.

3. **DOCUMENT EVERYTHING** – and include names, dates and times. By documenting the situation, you are actually doing three things. Firstly you are letting the other party know that you take the issue seriously. Secondly, you have a written record for future reference if memory fails or things are mis-stated at a later date. Finally, you can protect yourself if the conflict escalates to a higher authority.

4. **FOLLOW THE CONFLICT RESOLUTION PROCESS** – This is a tried and tested model that may be of value in a low level conflict scenario:

   - Listen to and document both sides of the conflict.
   - Talk to all parties separately to ascertain their version of the conflict.
   - Obtain suggestions for solutions from both parties independently of each other.
   - Bring the parties together to select a solution.
   - If this fails, escalate the issue to a higher authority.

5. **LEAVE IT AT THE DOOR** – Workplace conflict can cause issues outside of the workplace, affecting people's home and social lives. It is important to compartmentalise these conflict issues and leave them at work when you walk out the door, even if it is not as easy as it sounds.

6. **ESCALATE THE CONFLICT** – If you feel at all uncomfortable about the conflict or feel you or your associates (family and friends) might be in danger, escalate it to a higher authority. If they do not act, take it further. If safety is an issue, take it to your workplace security or the police.

CHAPTER SUMMARY

Communication needs to be applied in a considered manner for it to work effectively. It is essential that the communication is managed to maximise the return you gain from the time and effort you put into it.

Within teams and workplaces, many failed communication efforts can cause conflict situations and these should be carefully managed. A business is nothing without a team working together effectively to meet the needs of the customers, both internal and external.

The impact of poor communication is far reaching and can bring an otherwise successful business to its knees.

Chapter 3: Action Planning

In Chapter 1 we identified the need to have a plan for the management of your time.

In some cases you may be given a large activity or project to complete as part of your work duties. This activity will commonly have a number of phases and tasks to be completed within it.

Simple time management concepts may not be sufficient to integrate this activity or project into your work load.

When you are given your project or work activity, the first step is to clarify the details by generating a clear and concise goal. I suggest the use of the

SMART GOAL SETTING MODEL:

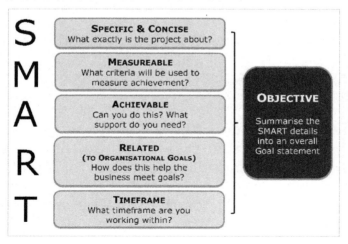

Case Study – SMART Goal Setting

Frank is given the task to conduct a HR review of each of his 10 team members, document the results, compile a summary of required professional development activities and report it all to management. This is due by the end of next week.

Frank uses the SMART goal formula to set his objective:

1. S – HR review to be conducted and reported to management.
2. M – 10 staff to be reviewed.
3. A –Pre-existing templates used from the office intranet.
4. R – Gaps in KPI performance and professional development requirements to be ascertained.
5. T – To be completed by 5pm next Friday.

Goal: To conduct a HR performance review on my 10 staff using existing templates, to identify performance gaps and report to management by 5pm next Friday (XX/XX/XXXX).

What needs to happen after defining the goal is the segmenting of the project or activity into chunks to make it more manageable for Frank. Each chunk can then be added into his work schedule, thus allowing for the time he will also require to complete any other work activities.

MIND-MAPPING TOOLS AND FLOW CHARTS

The use of a mind mapping tool or a flow chart allows you to put some structure into the project or activity.

It allows you to 'chunk' it into more achievable, smaller tasks. The example below reflects Frank's goal which was established on the previous page.

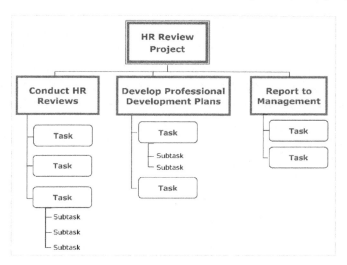

This flow chart would then allow you to develop an action plan with clearly defined tasks and dates which can easily be added to your work schedule at peak performance times.

Flow charts can easily be generated using Microsoft Word, Microsoft Publisher, Microsoft Visio or OpenOffice software. There are also numerous mind mapping software programs available online, some which require no up-front cost. In many cases there are some limits to the functionality in these versions. A program that I have used in the past is XMind. *Please take note that I am not recommending or endorsing any of these products. It is up to the user to do their own due diligence prior to the use of any software product.*

Once you have determined the flow of the tasks that need to be done, an 'Action Plan' should be created. A sample template for a versatile workplace action plan is depicted below. Note that there is space to include the costs of each activity as well as the resources required. This allows you to ascertain the costs involved in the project or activity and even potentially develop a budget for the activity.

Action Plan Template:

One issue that many people inadvertently face is what I call 'Action Plan Drift'. This is when you prepare a high quality, time framed action plan, which then goes into your 'In-Tray of Death', not to be seen until two days prior to the due date of the goal, when you have to work 18-hour days to make it happen.

ADD TASKS TO YOUR CALENDAR OR TO-DO LIST

Take every task that you have included on your action plan and put it onto your To-Do list or Outlook Calendar. Ensure you do not 'double-book' yourself with other activities from different areas of your role.

If you have multiple tasks scheduled for the same time, adjust either your action plan or calendar to ensure there is a block of time allocated to each task.

CHAPTER SUMMARY

Action planning is an essential tool to virtually every role. Medium to large scale activities require attention to detail and methods of tracking performance. Action plans provide both, and ensure that you achieve or exceed your goals. This is a strong recommendation for anyone looking to advance their career.

Chapter 4: You Are A Human Resource

There are a few core elements of HR Management that every employee should proactively apply to themselves.

> 1. Know and understand your Key Performance Indicators (KPIs).
>
> 2. Identify any gaps in your ability to achieve your KPIs.
>
> 3. Create a personal Professional Development Plan to ensure you can develop the skills and knowledge that you require to excel in your role.

KNOW AND UNDERSTAND YOUR KPIS

What is a KPI?

It is a measure or standard that you are expected to achieve as part of the performance of your work role.

As a business professional you should be acutely aware of what is expected of you. How can you achieve success if you do not know what your KPIs are?

Without that knowledge, you are setting yourself up to fail.

A KPI should be similar to a SMART goal or target. It must at the very least have some kind of quantifiable measurement by which you can gauge your success.

For Example:
A Salesperson may have a KPI to achieve 10 sales per week with a minimum average return of $10,000.

It is unlikely that you will have only 1 or 2 KPIs. There are usually at least 10 to 15 as part of any work role.

How can you find out what your KPIs are?

You should have been provided with a copy of them when you were employed or as your role has changed.

Many employers fail to update KPIs as people change roles. It is essential that you have a current list to be able to prove your worth to your organisation.

Ask your Manager, Team Leader or HR Representative for a copy of your KPIs. Give them a reasonable timeframe to provide you with the KPIs and follow up if you do not have them within that time.

Once you have your KPIs, read through them carefully. If you do not understand them, schedule a meeting with your Manager, Team Leader or HR Representative to discuss them. Ask for them to be rewritten if they are unclear.

Conduct Your Own KPI Analysis

There are two key questions that you should ask yourself when conducting a KPI Analysis:

1. What are the measureable criteria of each KPI?

2. What skills/abilities do I need to be able to achieve each KPI?

Complete this review using some sort of KPI Analysis template such as the example below:

Key Performance Indicator	Measureable Criteria?	I need more information on the Measureable Criteria:	Skills and Knowledge Required to Achieve KPI	I need to develop the following skills and knowledge:

It is a good idea to review this KPI Analysis with your Manager, Team Leader or HR Representative to ensure that you understand each KPI correctly and have made no misinterpretations.

GAPS IN SKILLS AND KNOWLEDGE

It is possible that you will have some gaps in the skills and knowledge that you will need to achieve your KPIs.

An option to consider is the use of a Professional Development Plan. Many organisations will do this as part of their regular HR Performance Reviews. If that is the case, then you may elect to align with the recommendations made at that point in time.

For those who are more proactive, (*this is usually seen as a positive and may put you on the 'possible promotion' radar of your Boss*), you may elect to develop your own Professional Development Plan.

Rank the development that you need in the following manner:

> 1. What skills do I need to develop as a priority? (i.e.: what is impeding significantly on my work performance?)

> 2. What can I develop quickly and remove from my list?

These will become your high priority development areas.

The next step is to create a professional development plan or strategy for each of the high priority skills and knowledge areas that require development.

PROFESSIONAL DEVELOPMENT PLAN TEMPLATE:

PROFESSIONAL DEVELOPMENT PLAN			
Performance Gap Identified:			
Possible rectifications/ options:			
Preferred Solution:			
Steps/tasks to close gap:	Proposed date	Completed	Date completed
		..	

Once you have completed your Professional Development plan, there are 2 options:

1. Undertake the development yourself and at your own expense.

2. Approach your Manager, Team Leader or HR Representative to implement a company sponsored professional development program.

CHAPTER SUMMARY

By considering yourself as a resource and conducting this style of HR review, you can identify ways to become a value-add to the business.

This proactive style of activity is generally seen as a considerable positive and may put you in good stead for ever increasing projects and job roles. This could lead to potential promotion and even the possibility of pay increases as time and performance progresses.

It is also essential to remember that simply conducting the analysis and identifying the gaps is not enough. You actually need to improve your performance and achieve the KPIs that you have been set as part of your job role.

Be the professional now that you want to be seen as in the future.

Chapter 5: Take A Quality Approach

One of the key success factors for any role is developing a clear definition of the quality expectations of your work activities.

The previous chapter on KPIs should have helped to identify your expected quality standards.

The perception of what is and is not an appropriate level of quality for your output varies from person to person. This can then lead to misinterpretation of goals and objectives by some key people and potential disappointment when the activity is completed.

HOW CAN YOU ESTABLISH WHAT THE ORGANISATION NEEDS?

The key steps to effectively defining quality in your role are consultation, documentation and commitment.

> 1. **CONSULT** with the appropriate Manager or higher authority until all of the quality parameters are fully understood by both parties;
>
> 2. **DOCUMENT** the parameters in a version controlled document, including as many details as possible; then,

3. Require all parties to formally **COMMIT** to and approve the quality expectations by signing off on the documentation, either electronically or in person.

This may appear as an extreme measure and in actuality you may not need to be as rigorous as this in your approach. The key outcome is simply to ensure you are completely clear on what is expected of you.

CONTINUOUS QUALITY IMPROVEMENT MINDSET

Once you achieve the quality standard required by your Manager, you have nothing further to develop, right?

Wrong!

To continue to develop your career and improve your skills and abilities, it is important that you develop a continuous quality improvement mindset.

You may have heard of it as the PDCA Cycle – Plan, Do, Check, Act. This is also known as the Deming Cycle.

(Look up W. Edwards Deming to thoroughly research this topic. It is the

type of understanding that sets you apart from your career competitors.)

The process always begins with Plan.   You then work through the four stages:

> 1. **PLAN** – Identify a genuine improvement that you can make.
>
> 2. **Do** – Implement the change.   This is usually done on a small scale to test the method.
>
> 3. **CHECK** – Review how the implementation went and identify any further areas of improvement or development.
>
> 4. **ACT** – If what you did in step 2 was successful, implement it in any other work areas that may benefit from it. If it was not successful, reassess it and go back to step 1.

It is important that you are continually asking what can be done better, faster, or in a simpler manner to save time, money and resources.

If you begin to ask this question about each activity that you do, you will develop ongoing improvements to a point where you are a high performing team member and an example of success to those around you.

This is what we refer to as a Continuous Improvement Mindset.

QUALITY IS NOT JUST ABOUT ACTIONS

Quality is about every aspect of your role. One of the key areas where quality fails in most organisations is that of communication.

Chapter 2 visited the concept of effective workplace communication.

My final thought on this topic is to **consider all of your communication activities as continuous improvement opportunities**. Here are some ideas you may be able to use in your role:

- Was that email written professionally and clearly?
- Did the report meet organisational document development guidelines?
- Am I using current templates for my documents?
- Should I be discussing xyz topic during work time?
- Do I make eye contact and speak clearly in meetings?
- Do I take notes when people are explaining things to me?
- Does my appearance communicate the role that I hold and my value of that role?

- Who can I network with inside of my organisation to make my role more effective?

Do not underestimate the power of continuous improvement in this area. After all, it is when you are a well-known, successful, respected and appreciated member of your team, that you will truly impress your Boss!

CHAPTER SUMMARY

Quality is a '*grey*' area. It is difficult to define and open to a vast array of alternative interpretations.

Your role is to deliver quality to either internal or external customers and your value to your employer is imbedded within your ability to deliver this effectively.

The core concept here it to ensure you and everyone around you are working with a common understanding as this will create team cohesion, respect and trust.

That is an environment that everyone would value being a part of.

Conclusion

It is easy to get tangled up in the day-to-day struggle that is your working life.

Whether you are that person who bounds out of bed, eager to start your work day, or you are the one who gets to your desk at one minute past your start time, you have a job to do for your employer and expectations of you are attached to that work.

The 37 tips outlined in this book will help you develop a passion for being a high performance team member, and assist you in seeing the value of implementing effective workplace behaviour.

Choose the tips and tools that can make the biggest difference to your working life and workplace reputation, and act on those first.

Ensure you make a plan to revisit your list of improvement opportunities and work through the rest. Don't wait until you have time – you never will.

Ask yourself if you would you rather be on a pathway of improvement and reputational advancement, or one of the drones? If the pathway to improvement is for you, than MAKE the time that you need to be the best that you can be!

The 37 Tips & Tools - Summarised

So What's Next?

Do Not Miss This Conference

PROJECT MANAGEMENT IN PLAIN ENGLISH CONFERENCE & TRAINING WORKSHOP

It is a hands-on project based program for everyday people who would like to excel in their role by developing a dynamic set of project management skills.

So a conference for everyone really!

It is also a pathway to complete the Nationally Recognised **Certificate IV in Project Management Practice** (BSB41515)

To find out more go to the website:
www.developmental.com.au/conference.html

JOIN US FOR OUR SERIES OF **20 FREE** WEBINARS

Each one lasts only 15 minutes and is packed with juicy tips and tools to help you at work.

Go to
www.developmental.com.au /events.html

References

- Fitzgerald, J, Fromholtz, M, Wood, , J & Zeffane, R 2006. *Organisational Behaviour: Core Concepts and Applications*. John Wiley & Sons, Milton.

Notes

Record notes and further research topics in the space provided below:

_____

_____

_____

_____

_____

_____

_____

_____

_____

_____

_____

Printed in Great Britain
by Amazon